NEWTON HALL
11/13

1 3 DEC 2013

3 1 MAR 2014
1 2 JAN 2015

Durham Clayport Library
1 1 MAY 2016

3 1 AUG 2016

- 4 DEC 2019

 **Durham** County Council Adults, Wellbeing and Health
Libraries, Learning and Culture

Please return or renew this item by the last date shown.
Fines will be charged if the book is kept after this date.
Thank you for using your library.

Renew online at www.durham.gov.uk/libraryonline

 **INTERWEAVE.**
interweave.com

Interweave grants permission to photocopy the templates in this publication for personal use.

The projects in this collection were originally published in other Interweave publications, including 101 Patchwork, Modern Patchwork, Quilt Scene, Quilting Arts, *and* Stitch *magazines. Some have been altered to update information and/or conform to space limitations.*

Interweave
A division of F+W Media, Inc.
201 East Fourth Street
Loveland, CO 80537
interweave.com

Manufactured in the United States by Versa Press

ISBN 978-1-62033-557-4 (pbk.)

Contents

Colorful Placemats

Modern Quilted Placemats

BY ALISSA HAIGHT CARLTON

These improvisational placemats sew up quickly and add a nice pop of color to any table setting. I was inspired to make my first set for my sister when we were having Christmas dinner at her house. With their simple but graphic patchwork design, these placemats are both warm and modern at the same time.

Materials

For four 14" × 19" (35.5 × 48.5 cm) placemats

- ☐ ⅜ yd (34 cm) of fabric A, cut 9½" × 24" (24 × 61 cm) (I used Bloom & Grow by My Mind's Eye for Riley Blake Designs.)

- ☐ ⅜ yd (34 cm) of fabric B, cut 10½" × 20" (26.5 × 51 cm) (I used Olive Kona Cotton.)

- ☐ ¼ yd (23 cm) of fabric C, cut 6½" × 28" (16.5 × 71 cm) (I used Cake Rock Beach Honeycomb in Green by Joelle Hoverson for Moda.)

- ☐ ¼ yd (23 cm) of fabric D, cut 8½" × 24" (21.5 × 61 cm) (I used Ice Frappe Kona Cotton.)

- ☐ Background fabric, ⅞ yd (80 cm) (I used Ash Kona Cotton), cut to the following sizes:

  - —Two 2¾" × 24" (7 × 61 cm) strips
  - —Two 2¼" × 20" (5.5 × 51 cm) strips
  - —Two 4¼" × 28" (11 × 71 cm) strips
  - —Two 3¼" × 24" (8.5 × 61 cm) strips

- ☐ Batting, four 14" × 19" (35.5 × 48.5 cm) pieces

- ☐ Backing fabric, four 14" × 19" (35.5 × 48.5 cm) pieces

- ☐ Binding fabric, eight strips 2½" (6.5 cm) × width of fabric

- ☐ Sewing machine and thread

- ☐ Iron and ironing board

I chose slightly different arrangements for each placemat. You can make them all identical if you'd like, but I find that making them somewhat different gives the set, as a whole, more interest. They are a matching group, yet each placemat is unique.

Please note that if you choose directional prints and are concerned with keeping the print upright, you might have to cut the rectangles differently. This will require you to buy more yardage.

Directions

1. Sew two of the background strips to each of Fabrics A through D, one along the top and one along the bottom, and press (**FIGURE 1**). Combine the fabrics and background strips as follows:

   —Fabric A with the 2¾" × 24" (7 × 61 cm) strips

   —Fabric B with the 2¼" × 20" (5.5 × 51 cm) strips

   —Fabric C with the 4¼" × 28" (11 × 71 cm) strips

   —Fabric D with the 3¼" × 24" (8.5 × 61 cm) strips

2. Cut each of the four rectangles of feature fabrics, now with the background fabric sewn on, into eight pieces as follows:

   Fabric A into 3" (7.5 cm) wide pieces (**FIGURE 2**)
   Fabric B into 2½" (6.5 cm) wide pieces
   Fabric C into 3½" (9 cm) wide pieces
   Fabric D into 3" (7.5 cm) wide pieces

3. Using two pieces of each feature fabric for one placemat, lay out the four placemat tops in a manner you find pleasing (**FIGURE 3**). I considered balancing the solid and patterned fabrics as I made my design decisions. I also knew that I didn't want my orange fabric against the edge since I was binding with that same fabric and didn't want the binding to blend in.

4. Sew together the eight pieces of fabric and press. Repeat for the remaining three placemat tops.

5. Layer and baste all four placemats, and quilt them as desired. To give a modern and clean look to the placemats, I did simple straight-line quilting, sewing vertical lines about ½" (1.3 cm) apart from each other.

6. Trim your quilted sandwich down to 14" × 19" (35.5 × 48.5 cm; it should already be the correct height, but it will be a bit wider than 19" [48.5 cm]). Keep your design in mind and try to trim evenly off of each side; take care not to cut too much off of one side or you will make one feature fabric noticeably narrower than the others.

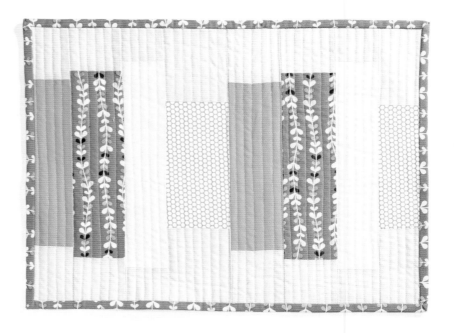

7 Bind all four placemats and give them as a gift to your favorite dinner-party throwing friend! 🖉

- - - - - - - - - - - - - - - - - - - -

ALISSA HAIGHT CARLTON has been obsessively quilting for several years. She is one of the founders of the Modern Quilt Guild and coauthored the book *Block Party.* She blogs at handmadebyalissa.com.

Improvisational Note

Feel free to adjust the height of any of the feature fabrics as desired. Want one to be taller or shorter? Not a problem—just make sure that the widths of the feature fabric and the two strips of background fabric add up to 15" (38 cm) before piecing. After they are pieced together, they will end up a perfect 14" (35.5 cm) tall.

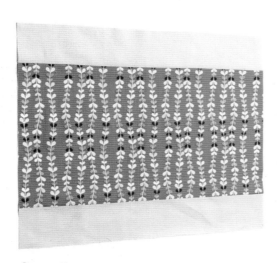

figure 1

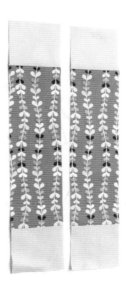

figure 2

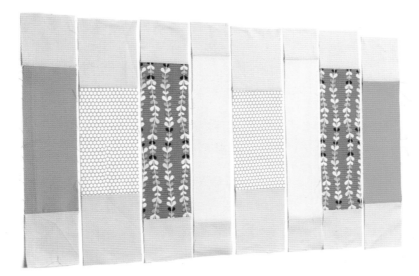

figure 3

Free-Motion Stitched Placemats

BY HELEN GREGORY

After seeing Jill Brummett Tucker's free-motion stitched pillows in *Quilting Arts Gifts* 2011/2012, I was inspired to play with the simple design of circles on squares, dressed up with a touch of free-motion stitching. While Jill's circles were created by over-dyeing and discharging fabrics using a Japanese dye process known as itajime, I elected to use commercial fabrics and fuse the circles to the background squares. The featured fabrics are from Moda's "Terrain" collection by Kate Spain.

Materials

For 4 placemats

□ Assorted prints for the background squares and circles, 3 yd (2.75 m) total

□ Fusible web, 2 yd (1.8 m)

□ Backing fabric, 1 yd (91.5 cm)

□ Low-loft batting, craft size

□ Rotary cutting supplies

□ Thread

□ Sewing machine with free-motion capabilities

□ Circle template

□ Stabilizer (optional)

Finished Size

13½" × 18" (34.5 × 45.5 cm)

Directions

1 From the assorted print fabrics, cut 96 squares 5" × 5" (12.5 × 12.5 cm) (half of these will be used for the circles).

2 From the backing fabric, cut 4 rectangles 14" × 18½" (35.5 × 47 cm). Also cut 4 rectangles 14" × 18½" (35.5 × 47 cm) from the batting. Set aside the batting and backing rectangles.

3 Using the circle pattern, trace 48 circles onto the paper side of the fusible web. Cut out the circles roughly, cutting outside the marked line.

4 Plan your fabric arrangement for each placemat, determining which fabrics will be the circles and which will be the background squares.

5 Following the manufacturer's instructions, iron a fusible web circle to the

Tip

+ Score the paper backing with a pin to be able to tear it and remove it from the fabric.

wrong side of each of the selected circle fabrics. Cut out the circles and remove the fusible backing.

6 Center each circle on the right side of a background square and fuse.

7 Free-motion stitch around the outer edge of each circle. Depending on the type of fabric and fusible web you're using, you may wish to use a layer of stabilizer for this step. You can use a tear-away stabilizer or a lightweight fusible stabilizer.

8 For each placemat, arrange the stitched squares into 3 rows of 4 squares each. Piece each row and press the seams in one direction. Sew the rows together.

9 Layer each placemat as follows: batting rectangle, placemat top (right-side up), backing rectangle (right-side down). Using a ¼" (6 mm) seam allowance, stitch around the outside edge, leaving a 6" (15 cm) opening along one of the long sides.

10 Clip the corners, turn the placemat right-side out, and press. Turn the raw edges of the opening to the inside and press. Topstitch ⅛" (3 mm) from the edge around the entire placemat. Complete the remaining placemats in the same manner.

11 To finish, quilt in the ditch (or as desired). 🍃

HELEN GREGORY is the vice president of content for Interweave.

FREE-MOTION STITCHED PLACEMATS
Circle Template

(template is actual size)

Personalized Placemats

BY KRISTA FLECKENSTEIN

When my daughters were young and tasked with setting the table for dinner, their favorite part of the chore was choosing where each of us would sit each night. To make it simple, I designed these personalized placemats featuring each family member's favorite color and fabrics. Setting the table is now fun and easy! These placemats are a quick sew—you can get them from your cutting table to the dinner table in an afternoon.

Materials

For 4 placemats

☐ Natural linen, ¾ yd (68.5 cm)

☐ 8 accent fabrics, 2 coordinating strips 1½" × 14" (3.8 × 35.5 cm) for each placemat

☐ 4 backing fabrics, 4 rectangles 15" × 20" (38 × 51 cm)

☐ 4 binding fabrics, ¼ yd (23 cm) each

☐ Low-loft batting, 4 rectangles 15" × 20" (38 × 51 cm)

☐ Rotary cutting supplies

☐ Spray starch (optional)

Finished Size

12" × 17" (30.5 × 43 cm)

Directions

1. From the linen, cut 4 rectangles 13" × 17" (33 × 43 cm).

2. Along the top long side of each linen rectangle, mark 4½" (11.5 cm) (A) and 6½" (16.5 cm) (B) from the left edge **(FIGURE 1)**.

3. Along the bottom long side of each linen rectangle, mark 4" (10 cm) (C) and 7½" (19 cm) (D) from the left edge **(FIGURE 2)**.

4. Using a rotary cutter and a ruler, cut a straight line from point A to point C **(FIGURE 3)**.

5. Sew your first 1½" × 14" (3.8 × 35.5 cm) accent strip between the 2 pieces of linen, using a ¼" (6 mm) seam allowance **(FIGURE 4)**. Press.

Tip

+ Placemats require frequent laundering. Prewash the fabrics to prevent shrinkage.

Tip

+ Linen can be very shifty. Stabilize it with spray starch to make cutting much easier.

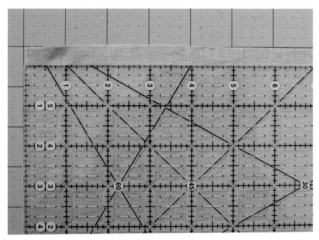

figure 1

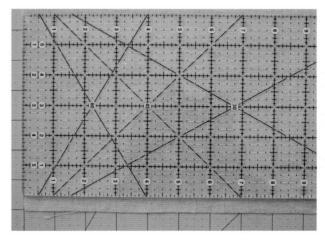

figure 2

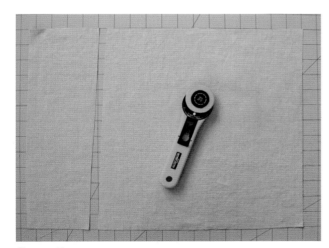

figure 3

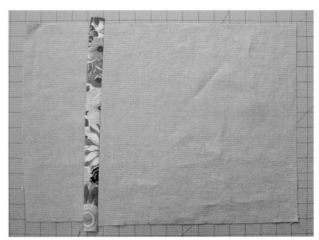

figure 4

6 Using a rotary cutter and a ruler, cut a straight line from point B to point D **(FIGURE 5)**.

7 Sew the coordinating accent strip between the 2 pieces of linen, using a ¼" (6 mm) seam allowance **(FIGURE 6)**. Press.

8 Layer each placemat as follows: backing (right-side down), batting, and pieced front (right-side up). Baste.

9 Quilt as desired **(FIGURE 7)**.

10 Trim to 12" × 17" (30.5 × 43 cm) **(FIGURE 8)**.

11 Bind.

12 Repeat Steps 1–11 to complete the other 3 placemats. 🌿

- -

Visit **KRISTA FLECKENSTEIN**'s blog at spottedstone.blogspot.com.

Tip
- - - - - - - - - - - - - - - -

+ Don't worry if your placemat edges don't line up perfectly. The measurements for piecing are generous to allow room for error. You will trim the finished placemats to size after quilting.

figure 5

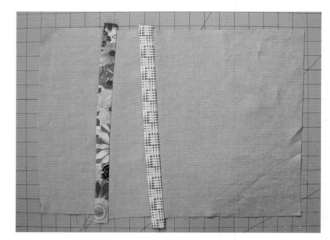

figure 6

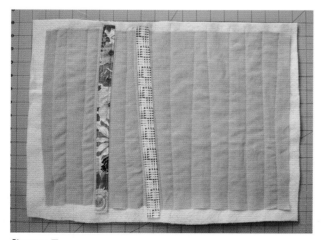

figure 7

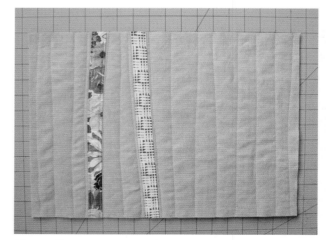

figure 8

Nametag Placemats

BY KEVIN KOSBAB

Show your guests where to sit with personalized placemats based on the ubiquitous "Hello, My Name Is . . ." nametag. Self-stick felt letters and large-stitch handquilting make them easy enough to sew up one for each family member.

Materials

(for 1 placemat)

- ☐ ½ yd (46 cm) of 45" (115 cm) wide solid red or blue cotton (Main)
- ☐ ¼ yd (23 cm) of 45" (115 cm) wide solid white cotton
- ☐ Coordinating sewing thread
- ☐ 1" (2.5 cm) self-adhesive felt letters (see Notes)
- ☐ 2" (5 cm) self-adhesive felt letters (see Notes)
- ☐ 18¼" × 13¼" (46.5 × 33.5 cm) piece of cotton batting
- ☐ Black pearl cotton
- ☐ Drinking glass or other round object (to use as a guide for rounding corners)
- ☐ Water-soluble fabric marking pen
- ☐ Hand-embroidery needle
- ☐ Nametag Placemat template on page 15

Finished Size

18" × 13" (46 × 33 cm)

Notes

✳ All seam allowances are ¼" (6 mm) unless otherwise indicated.

✳ For explanations of terms and techniques, see Sewing Basics.

✳ Self-adhesive felt letters, stocked by craft supply stores, make this a quick project. You'll need enough 2" (5 cm) letters to spell "HELLO" and enough 1" (2.5 cm) letters for "MY NAME IS." You may want to consider applying a permanent fabric adhesive to the back of the felt letters before applying them to the fabric, to provide a more lasting bond. If you'd like an even more durable placemat, trace letters from the template onto white fabric and appliqué them by hand or machine. The smaller letters could be machine satin-stitched.

✳ Knots from the pearl-cotton quilting will show on the back of the placemat. To conceal them, cut the back rectangle from black cotton instead of the Main color or sew a nonslip pad to the back of the placemat after quilting.

✳ Spot-clean placemats as necessary; do not machine wash.

Cut Fabric

1. Cut 2 rectangles for the front of the placemat from the Main fabric, one measuring 18½" (47 cm) long × 4½" (11.5 cm) wide and the other 18½" (47 cm) long × 1½" (3.8 cm) wide. Cut another rectangle for the back measuring 18½" (47 cm) long × 13½" (34.5 cm) wide.

2. Cut a rectangle for the name field from the white cotton, measuring 18½" (47 cm) long × 8½" (21.5 cm) wide.

Make Placemat Front

3. With right sides together and 18½" (47 cm) sides aligned, sew one of the front Main pieces to the white piece. Sew the remaining front Main piece to the opposite edge of the white piece. Press the seam allowances toward the Main fabric.

4. Fold the pieced front in half widthwise and finger-press a crease in the wider Main piece to indicate the center. Open the piece up and place it over the template, aligning the fold with the dotted line on the pattern and the seam with the dashed line. Use a light box or bright window, if necessary, to see the pattern markings through the fabric.

5. Peel the paper backings off the felt letters and adhere them to the Main fabric, using the template as a rough guide for placement. The shapes of your letters may not match the template exactly, but use the template to keep the lines straight and spacing even. Start from the middle of each line of text and work outward to make sure the lines are centered.

Assemble Placemat

6. Using a drinking glass, spray bottle, or other round object as a guide, draw a curve ¼" (6 mm) inside each corner of the back Main piece, on the wrong side, to create an evenly rounded guide for sewing.

7. Center the pieced front on the batting, embellished-side up, then place the backing on top, marked-side up (the front and back are right sides together). Pin all layers together.

8. Sew around the perimeter of the placemat, leaving an 8"–10" (20.5–25.5 cm) opening near the center of the bottom edge. At the corners, sew on the marked curves, pivoting gradually and repeatedly to make a smooth curve that meets the next side at the ¼" (6 mm) seam allowance.

9. Trim the excess fabric at the corners to a ¼" (6 mm) seam allowance, then clip the curved seam allowances to reduce bulk at the corners. Turn the placemat right-side out through the opening.

10. Press the seam allowances to the wrong side at the opening so the bottom edge is straight. Edgestitch all the way around the perimeter of the placemat, making sure the bottom opening is sewn shut.

Quilt Placemat

11. Stitch in the ditch between the pieces of the front to stabilize the placemat.

12. Write a name in large letters across the white piece of the front with a water-soluble fabric marking pen. Using pearl cotton, handquilt along the markings with a closely spaced running stitch.

13. Clip thread ends to tidy the back of the placemat and lightly dampen the front to remove markings (or refer to pen manufacturer's instructions). 🖋

KEVIN KOSBAB is a freelance writer, an editor, and a pattern designer. Find his Feed Dog Designs patterns in stores and on the Web at feeddog.net.

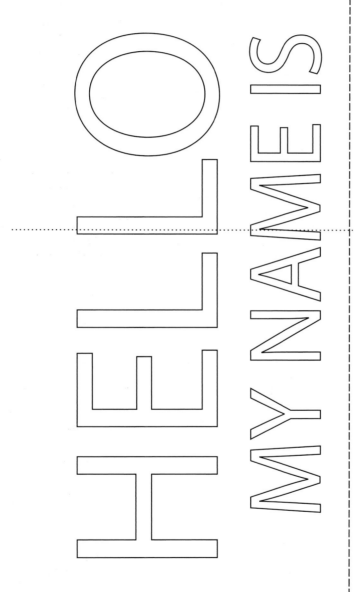

Nametag template
Enlarge template 125%

Graphic
Table Runners

Fizz Table Runner

BY LISA COX

Interlocking circles have been elegantly embroidered sashiko style onto natural linen to create this elegant table runner. Hand screen-printed organic cotton on the borders and backing echo the handstitched patterning.

Materials

□ 1 yd (91.5 cm) of printed cotton (shown: brown and cream print; see Notes)

□ ½ yd (46 cm) of medium-weight natural linen (see Notes)

□ ½ yd (46 cm) of medium-weight fusible interfacing

□ Pearl cotton, size 5 (shown: DMC 938 Chocolate)

□ Embroidery needle

□ Rotary cutter, rigid acrylic ruler, and self-healing mat (optional, for cutting)

□ Water-soluble fabric marking pen

□ Serger (optional)

□ Point turner (or similar tool such as a chopstick)

□ Fizz Table Runner embroidery template on page 19

Finished Size

13" × 35" (33 × 89 cm)

Notes

* All seam allowances are ¼" (6 mm) unless otherwise noted.

* For explanations of terms and techniques, see Sewing Basics.

* The print fabric used in the sample is Pippijoe Daisies Chocolate, hand screen-printed on organic cotton by Australian textile designer Caitlin Klooger. Find her fabrics at pippijoe.com.

* The linen used in the sample is unprimed artist's linen. Check with your local art supply store or danielsmith.com or utrecht.com.

* Preclean the fabric using the same method that you plan to clean the finished table runner. If your interfacing is nonwoven, you do not need to pretreat it. However, you do need to preshrink woven interfacing to prevent puckers after the first laundering. To preshrink woven interfacing, soak it for about 10 minutes in a basin of warm water and lay it flat on a towel to dry.

* Test your fabric marker on a scrap of the fabric to make sure the markings can be easily removed according to the manufacturer's instructions.

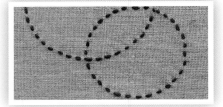

Assemble the Table Runner

5 With right sides together, pin a 6½" × 13½" (16.5 × 34.5 cm) cotton rectangle to one short end of the embroidered linen panel. Stitch in place and press the seam allowance toward the cotton. Topstitch ⅛" (3 mm) from the seam to secure the seam allowance. Repeat with the other cotton rectangle on the other end of the linen panel.

6 Fuse the interfacing to the wrong side of the assembled table runner top, following the manufacturer's instructions. Pin the table runner top to the backing with right sides together. Stitch around the perimeter, leaving a 5" (12.5 cm) opening on one of the short sides for turning right-side out.

7 Trim the corners diagonally and turn right-side out through the opening. Push out the corners with a point turner or chopstick. Turn the seam allowances at the opening to the inside, then press the table runner flat. Edgestitch around the perimeter, which will close the opening. ✎

- -

LISA COX is an occupational therapist by day and an avid crafter at night. Her designs have appeared in many books and magazines. Lisa lives in Perth, Australia. She collaborates with her daughter, Sarah, on their blog, spoonfullofsugargirls.blogspot.com.

Embroider the Linen Panel

1 From the natural linen, cut one 26" × 15" (66 × 38 cm) rectangle. Serge or zigzag the raw edges on all four sides.

2 Trace the provided embroidery template onto the linen using a water-soluble fabric pen. Use a light table or a window if necessary to see the template through the linen. If you prefer, you can use three different-size circle templates or other circular objects to create a custom design.

3 Using the pearl cotton and embroidery needle, handstitch the circles with a sashiko stitch, which is similar to a running stitch. Instead of the stitches being of equal length on the right and wrong sides of the fabric, a sashiko stitch has longer stitches on the right side and shorter stitches on the wrong side. Remove the water-soluble pen markings following the manufacturer's instructions. Press the linen flat. Trim the linen rectangle to 24" × 13½" (61 × 34.5 cm).

Cut the Fabric

4 From the printed cotton, cut:

—Two 6½" × 13½" (16.5 × 34.5 cm) rectangles for each end of the table runner

—One 13½" × 35½" (34.5 × 90 cm) rectangle for the table runner backing

From the interfacing, cut:

—One 13½" × 35½ " (34.5 × 90 cm) rectangle

fizz table runner
embroidery template

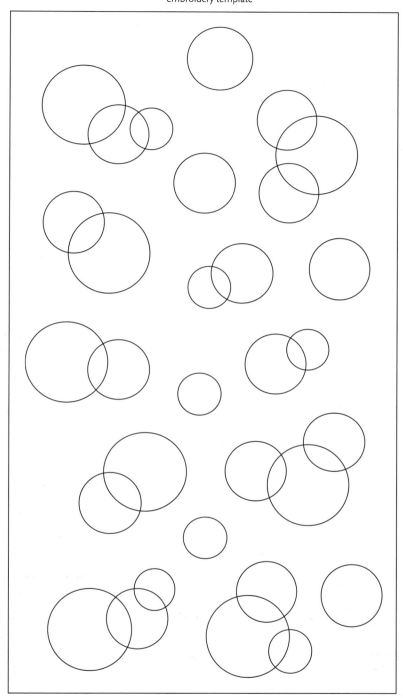

Enlarge template 300%

Reflected Wedges Table Runner

BY JACQUIE GERING

Traditional Dresden Plate wedges come together in a new way to create a delightfully modern feeling table runner. Echo quilting in the wedges adds a polished finish.

Materials

☐ Wedge template on page 23

☐ Template plastic or cardboard

☐ 15 assorted gray and yellow print fabrics, 1 rectangle 4" × 14" (10 × 35.5 cm) from each

☐ Solid yellow fabric for divider strips and binding, ½ yd (46 cm)

☐ Rotary cutting supplies

☐ Backing fabric, ¾ yd (68.5 cm)

☐ Low-loft cotton batting, 18" × 46" (45.5 × 117 cm) piece

☐ Basting safety pins

☐ Tape

☐ Design wall (optional)

Finished Size

40½" × 13" (103 × 33 cm)

Directions

All seams are ¼" (6 mm) unless otherwise indicated.

1 Trace the wedge pattern onto template plastic or cardboard; cut out. Be sure to trace and cut accurately.

2 Gather the 15 print rectangles and use the wedge template to cut 15 wedges.

3 From the solid yellow fabric, cut 7 strips 1" (2.5 cm) × WOF (width of fabric). Subcut these into 14 strips 1" × 16" (2.5 × 40.5 cm).

4 Arrange the 15 wedges in a row on your design wall, alternating the short and long ends of the wedges. Placing different values next to each other will create more interest and movement in your table runner (FIGURE 1).

5 When you are satisfied with the arrangement of the prints, pin a yellow strip, right sides together, to the right side of each wedge. The strip will extend beyond the edges of the wedge (FIGURE 2). Sew, and press the seam toward the wedge. Do this for all the wedges except for the final wedge in the row.

6 Place the wedges back in order on the design wall.

7 Sew the wedges together in order from left to right to create a panel, placing right sides together and matching raw edges. To help line up the wedges for sewing, place 2 wedges side by side. Place a pin where the right corner of the first wedge meets the left corner of the second wedge as shown in FIGURE 3.

8 Place the second wedge right-side down on the first wedge, aligning the corner of the wedge with the pin (FIGURE 4). Sew, and press the seam toward the wedge.

9 Repeat to create a panel of wedges.

Process photos by Jacquie Gering

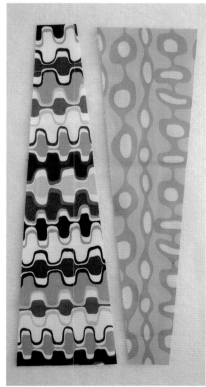

figure 1

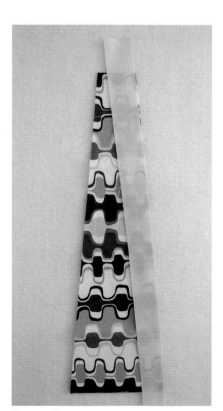

figure 2

figure 3

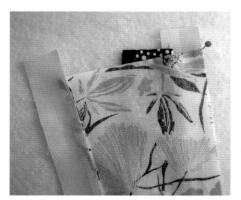

figure 4

10 Place the panel of wedges on your cutting mat and trim the panel to 13" (33 cm) wide, making sure the top and bottom edges of the panel are parallel.

11 Align the top of the panel with a horizontal line on the cutting mat. Trim the ends of the panel so that they are perpendicular to the top and bottom of the panel (**FIGURE 5**).

12 From the backing fabric, cut 1 strip 17" × 40" (43 × 101.5 cm) and 1 strip 17" × 6½" (43 × 16.5 cm). Sew the 2 strips together along the 17" (43 cm) side. Press the seam to the side to finish the backing.

13 Press the backing and place it wrong-side up on a flat surface. Tape the 4 sides of the backing to the flat surface, making sure it is taut but not stretched. Center the batting on top of the backing, making sure there are no wrinkles. Then place the table runner top right-side up on the batting, centering it.

14 Baste the quilt sandwich with safety pins.

15 Machine or hand quilt the layers together as desired, removing the safety pins as you quilt. The featured table runner is machine quilted with echo quilting within each wedge.

16 Trim the batting and backing even with the top to prepare it for binding. From the solid yellow fabric, cut 3 strips 2¼" (5.5 cm) × WOF. Join the binding strips. Press the binding in half lengthwise with wrong sides together to create double-fold binding. Follow the instructions under Binding with Mitered Corners in Sewing Basics to bind the quilt. Place the runner on your table and enjoy! 🌿

- -

Visit **JACQUIE GERING**'s blog at tallgrassprairiestudio.blogspot.com.

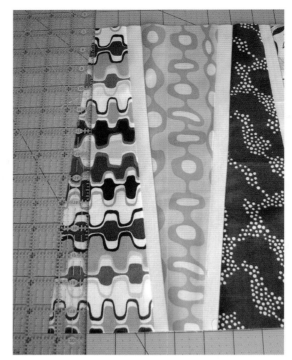

figure 5

Adjusting the Size of Your Table Runner

This runner can be easily customized for the size of your table. Make it wider by using a longer wedge template, or shorten or lengthen it by subtracting or adding wedges.

REFLECTED WEDGES TABLE RUNNER
Wedge Template

**Enlarge
200%**

Plaid Curves Table Runner

BY KEVIN KOSBAB

Contrast the linear graphic lines of plaid by piecing wedges into color-coordinated curves (with no curved piecing) for a clever spin on a traditional quilt block. The quilt stitching extends the plaid pattern into the background for added visual interest.

Materials

- ☐ ⅜ yd (34.5 cm) of 45" (114.5 cm) wide cotton (Foundation 1; shown: golden brown)

- ☐ ⅜ yd (34.5 cm) of 45" (114.5 cm) wide cotton print (Foundation 2; shown: golden brown print)

- ☐ Assorted scraps of plaid fabrics, each at least 4" × 8½" (10 × 21.5 cm), in 4 color groupings (groupings shown: blues, greens, turquoises, reds; you'll need enough for 24 wedges; see Notes and Wedge template)

- ☐ ½ yd (46 cm) of 45" (114.5 cm) wide backing fabric

- ☐ ⅔ yd (61 cm) of 45" (114.5 cm) wide binding fabric

- ☐ Paper for template

- ☐ Masking tape or other low-tack tape

- ☐ Freezer paper

- ☐ Sewing thread in several coordinating colors

- ☐ 15" × 48" (38 × 122 cm) rectangle of low-loft batting

- ☐ Invisible monofilament thread (optional)

- ☐ Pinking shears

- ☐ Spray starch and paintbrush

- ☐ Safety pins or quilt-basting spray

- ☐ Walking foot for sewing machine

- ☐ Water-soluble fabric-marking pen

- ☐ Plaid Curves Table Runner templates on page 27

Finished Size

11½" × 44½" (29 × 113 cm)

Notes

- * All seam allowances are ¼" (6 mm) unless otherwise noted.

- * For explanations of terms and techniques, see Sewing Basics.

- * Sample shows plaids in related colors for each of the four blocks in the runner. You could also make each curve a gradation from light to dark or from one color to another; you'll need six wedges in each color grouping, but it's okay to repeat fabrics.

- * Press all seams open unless otherwise noted. This will make it easier to turn the edges of the pieced curves.

- * When starting a line of quilting in the middle of the runner (i.e., a line that won't be crossed when the binding is attached), sew about ¼" (6 mm) of very short stitches (length 0.3–0.4 mm) rather than backtacking, then change to your normal stitch length. Shorten the stitch length again at the end of the quilted line if it is also in the middle of the runner.

Prepare the Templates

1. Trace the Wedge template (page 27) onto a piece of paper. Cut the traced template out carefully, retaining the "window" left in the paper when the template is cut out for Step 4. Stick a few rolled-up pieces of tape onto the back of the template and set aside.

2. Trace the Curve template (page 27) onto the paper side of the freezer paper. Be sure to transfer the dashed lines to the freezer paper as well. Cut the traced template out along the solid lines. Make four.

Cut the Fabric

3. Cut four 11½" × 11½" (29 × 29 cm) foundation squares from the Foundation fabrics. For variety, sample shows a solid cotton for three of the foundations and a print for the other, but you can cut all four from ⅔ yd (61 cm) of a single fabric if you prefer.

4. Use the Wedge template "window" to choose portions of plaid that look appealing in the narrow wedge. Make sure the prominent lines of the plaid run the length of the wedge, perpendicular to the shorter ends. Place the Wedge template in the window, pressing to adhere the tape to the fabric, and remove the window frame. Trace the template onto the fabric and cut out. Follow this process to cut six plaid wedges from each color grouping of assorted scraps for a total of 24 wedges. Handle the wedges carefully to avoid stretching the bias edges.

5. Cut a crosswise strip 14" (35.5 cm) wide from the backing fabric. Cut this strip in half along the lengthwise grain, creating two 14" (35.5 cm) wide rectangles, and remove the selvedges.

6. Cut a 6" × 14" (15 × 35.5 cm) backing insert from the binding fabric.

7. Cut five bias strips, each 2" (5 cm) wide, from the remaining binding fabric, to total at least 122" (310 cm).

Join the Plaid Wedges

8. On a flat surface, arrange the six wedges from each plaid color grouping with long sides adjoining to make a quarter-circle curve resembling the Curve template.

9. With right sides together, sew the long edges of two adjacent wedges together. Continue joining wedges to this unit until the color grouping is complete. Press flat, taking care not to stretch the bias edges. Repeat to join the wedges for each color grouping.

Appliqué the Curves

10. Place the shiny side of a freezer-paper Curve template onto the wrong side of one pieced group of wedges. The fabric should extend equally past the template along the curved sides. Align the dashed lines with the seams and press the template in place with a hot, dry iron.

11. Trim the excess fabric ⅜" (1 cm) from the curved edges with pinking shears. Clip into this seam allowance on both curves, almost to the template.

12. Spray a small amount of starch into the cap from the spray starch can. Brush the starch onto the curved seam allowances with a paintbrush or finger, moistening only the fabric, not the freezer paper. Press the allowances over the freezer paper, making sure the fabric wraps closely around the template's curved edges. Press until the starch is dry. If the curves are not smooth, moisten the seam allowance, reshape, and press

again. Remove the template when the fabric has cooled and press once more to set the pressed edges.

13 Repeat Steps 10–12 to turn the edges of each plaid curve.

14 Pin each plaid curve onto the right side of a foundation square, aligning the raw edges. The inside curve should lie 4⅜" (11.3 cm) from the corner along the side of the square.

15 Topstitch ⅛" (3 mm) from each curve to attach the fans to the foundations, using a thread that blends into the plaid colors.

Assemble the Runner

16 Arrange the appliquéd fan blocks in two pairs, orienting adjacent blocks to create a semicircle. With right sides together, sew the seam joining each pair of blocks. Rotate one pair 180 degrees, so the fan centers face in opposite directions, and join the two pairs to complete the runner top (see the photo on page 24). Press flat.

17 Sew one backing rectangle to each 14" (35.5 cm) side of the backing insert. Press.

18 With the backing wrong-side up, center the batting on top, then center the assembled runner top right-side up to create a quilt sandwich. Baste the three layers together with safety pins or basting spray. If using safety pins, pin in rows, spacing pins no more than 6" (15 cm) apart.

Quilt and Finish

19 With coordinating or invisible thread and a walking foot on your sewing machine, stitch in the ditch along the plaid curves, through all layers.

20 Using a fabric-marking pen and a ruler, extend the seam lines between the plaid wedges outward to the block edges and inward across the center semicircles. Quilt along these lines with invisible or coordinating thread, also stitching along the seams between the wedges.

21 Choose a few lines (suggested: narrow, bold lines) from the pattern of each plaid wedge to extend outward from the top (larger) curve. Use the marking pen and ruler to extend the lines from the wide end of the wedge to the block raw edge. With thread that matches the line color in the plaid, quilt from the narrow end of the wedge to the edge of the block, following the plaid line and its extension. Distribute marked and quilted lines evenly across the runner.

22 Square up the runner, trimming the batting and backing to match the runner top. Join the bias binding strips into a continuous length with diagonal seams (see Sewing Basics). Press the binding in half, lengthwise, with wrong sides together. Follow the instructions under Binding with Mitered Corners in Sewing Basics to bind the runner edges with the single-fold binding. 🖋

- -

KEVIN KOSBAB regularly designs modern quilts and sewing projects for *Stitch* and other magazines. Find his Feed Dog Designs patterns in stores and on the Web at feeddog.net.

**Enlarge both templates
155%**

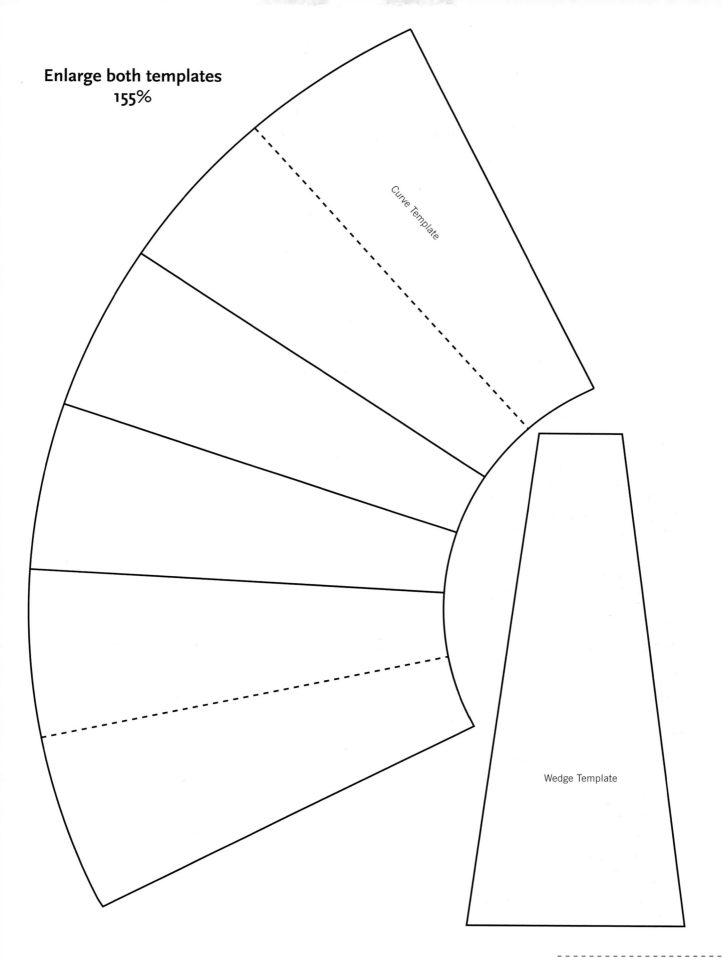

Curve Template

Wedge Template

Hip Squares Table Runner

BY JOSÉE CARRIER

Bring the summer indoors with this colorful table runner. Use bold solids to make a patchwork of overlapping diamonds, then insert a hint of your jazziest prints. A neutral linen background will make the whole design sparkle.

Materials

☐ ¼ yd (23 cm) bold solid color cotton fabric for each of the 2 end squares and details in the binding and back panel (shown: green and darker aqua, fabrics A and D)

☐ ¼ yd (23 cm) of a bold solid color cotton fabric for each of the 2 central squares and details in the binding and back panel (shown: orange and lighter aqua, fabrics B and C)

☐ 1 yd (91.5 cm) of a print cotton fabric for back panel and the 3 squares where the diamonds overlap (shown: red floral print, fabric F)

☐ 1⅛ yd (103 cm) of a neutral solid fabric (shown: linen/cotton blend in natural, fabric L)

☐ 18" × 64" (45.5 × 162.5 cm) piece of low-loft batting

☐ Coordinating thread

☐ Quilting thread in coordinating color (shown: natural)

☐ Handsewing needle

☐ Rotary cutter, rigid acrylic rulers, and self-healing mat

☐ Quilter's safety pins or quilt basting spray

☐ Walking foot or even-feed foot (optional)

☐ Blue painter's tape

Finished Size

15" × 60" (38 × 152.5 cm)

Notes

✳ Yardage requirements are based on 44" (112 cm) wide fabric.

✳ The print cotton fabric chosen for the overlapping squares will be fussy-cut to have the printed motif properly placed in the square. Choose fabric so that the design will properly fit a finished 4" (10 cm) square.

✳ Ideal ruler sizes are a 6" × 24" (15 × 61 cm) and a 12½" (31.5 cm) square.

✳ A walking foot prevents different fabric layers from shifting while quilting.

✳ Fussy-cut the print cotton fabric for the overlapping squares on the grain or on the bias depending on which orientation fits the print best.

✳ Unless otherwise noted, sew all pieces with right sides together using a ¼" (6 mm) seam allowance. Press all seams open. The ¼" (6 mm) seam allowance is particularly important for good alignment of the solid color squares' edges.

Cut the Fabric

1 For each of the 2 central squares, cut:

—1 piece of 5½" × 4½" (14 × 11.5 cm) (B1 and C1)

—1 piece of 9½" × 1½" (24 × 3.8 cm) (B2 and C2)

2 For each of the 2 end squares, cut:

—1 piece of 9½" × 5½" (24 × 14 cm) (A1 and D1)

—1 piece of 5½" × 4½" (14 × 11.5 cm) (A2 and D2)

3 From each of the 4 bold solid color cottons used for the squares, cut:

—1 piece of 7½" × 2½" (19 × 6.5 cm) for the back panel (A3, B3, C3, and D3)

—2 pieces of 2½" × 2" (6.5 × 5 cm) to use as details in the binding (A4, B4, C4, and D4)

4 Cut the print cotton fabric in half lengthwise (2 pieces, each 36" × 22" [91.5 × 56 cm]). From those pieces, fussy-cut three 4½" (11.5 cm) squares for the overlapping squares on the front (F1). Cut these at the end of the pieces. Be sure to have remaining pieces of at least 30" × 22" (76 × 56 cm) (F2).

5 From the neutral solid color fabric, cut the following pieces for the front panel:

—2 pieces of 9½" × 22" (14 × 20.5 cm) (L1)

—2 pieces of 5½" × 8" (14 × 20.5 cm) (L2)

—2 pieces of 5½" × 10" (14 × 25.5 cm) (L3)

—6 pieces of 4½" × 7" (11.5 × 18 cm) (L4)

—4 pieces of 1½" × 8" (3.8 × 20.5 cm) (L5)

6 From the same fabric, cut:

—2 pieces of 7½" × 7" (19 × 18 cm) (L6) for the back panel

—4 strips, each 2½" (6.5 cm) wide across the width of the fabric for the binding

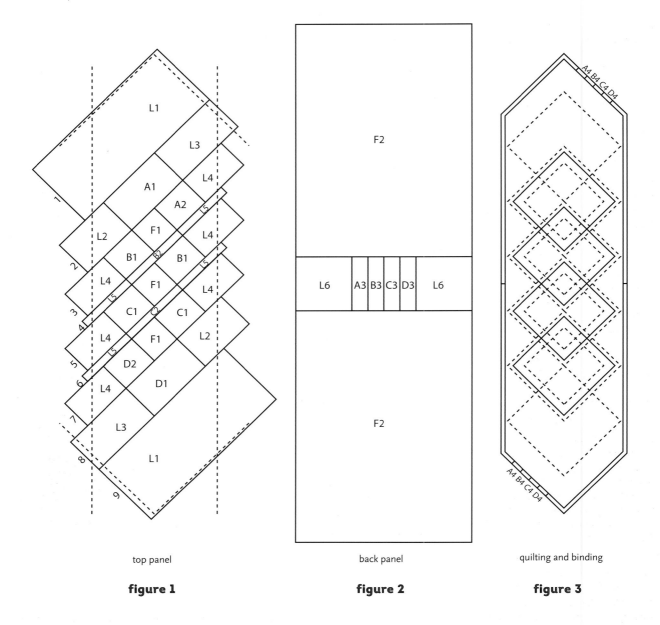

top panel

figure 1

back panel

figure 2

quilting and binding

figure 3

Assemble the Top Panel

7 Following **FIGURE 1**, assemble all pieces of Row 2. Do the same for Rows 3–8.

8 Pin and sew Rows 1 and 2 by aligning their left edges. Add Row 3 by aligning the seam lines of the first solid color square (fabric A). Keep adding the rows by aligning the seam lines of the common solid color squares. For Row 9, align the left edge with the left edge of Row 8.

9 Trim the top panel on the right using your rotary cutter and long acrylic ruler by aligning the ruler 1½" (3.8 cm) from the right corner of the solid linen squares. Repeat on the left side.

10 Trim the top panel's ends using the 12½" (31.5 cm) square acrylic ruler. Position it at a 45-degree angle and align the corners in a straight line with the corners of the solid linen squares at 12½" (31.5 cm) from the top corner. Repeat for the bottom end.

Assemble the Back Panel

11 Following the construction diagram for the back panel, assemble all pieces of the center row together (**FIGURE 2**).

12 Pin and sew both large pieces of the print cotton fabric (fabric F) on each side of the center row.

Prepare the Binding

13 Take one of the 2½" × 2" (6.5 × 5 cm) pieces from each of the solid color cottons (A4, B4, C4, and D4) and assemble them in a continuous strip by sewing their 2½" (6.5 cm) wide edges together (**FIGURE 3**).

14 On each side, sew one of the 2½" (6.5 cm) wide strips from the neutral solid color fabric (fabric L). Repeat pieced binding in Step 13 to make a pieced binding for the other edge of the table runner.

Fold the binding sections in half lengthwise and press it to create a continuous double-layer binding (see Sewing Basics).

Finish the Table Runner

15 Mark the center of the Back Panel's middle row by placing straight pins on the left and right edges. Do the same at the top and bottom edges by aligning the pins with the seam of pieces B3 and C3 (**FIGURE 3**). Mark the center of the Top Panel as well on the left and right edges by placing pins where the center solid color squares meet. Use the end tips for the top and bottom. This will help align the quilt sandwich.

16 Lay the Back Panel, wrong-side up, on a flat surface. Center the batting on top. Place the Top Panel, right-side up, by aligning the top and back panel centers. Baste the three layers together with safety pins or basting spray. If using safety pins, place them 4"–6" (10–15 cm) apart.

17 Thread your sewing machine with thread that coordinates with the top panel and, ideally, a walking foot. For each solid color square, quilt a 7" (18 cm) inner square 1" (2.5 cm) from the edge and a 10" outer square that is ½" (1.3 cm) from the edge. Quilt two additional 10" (25.5 cm) squares with corners meeting with previous quilting squares at the center of top and bottom solid color squares (**FIGURE 3**). Use painter's tape as a guide to mark each square for quilting. Start quilting on one of the edges. Bring the bobbin thread on top and backstitch or sew a few short stitches to secure the threads. Continue and clip the threads once the walking foot is out of the way. When you reach a corner, bring the needle down and lift the foot to turn the fabric. Once you are back to the starting point, continue for a few stitches and

A strip-pieced center and large floral print add unexpected elements to this reversible table runner.

secure the threads in the same manner. Remove the painter's tape.

18 Trim excess fabric from back panel and batting even with the top panel to prepare for binding.

19 Refer to the instructions under Binding with Mitered Corners option B in Sewing Basics to bind the edges of the table runner. Before sewing, align the striped band of each binding strip at one end of the table runner. For the first one, align it with the middle of the table runner's top right edge; for the second, align it with the middle of the bottom left edge (**FIGURE 3**). Position and pin both binding

strips all around and join at the center of the table runner on both sides. For mitered corners larger than 90 degrees, fold the binding in the same manner so that its edge aligns with the next edge to bind. 🍃

- - - - - - - - - - - - - - - - - - - -

JOSÉE CARRIER has been working in the engineering field. She is currently a mom at home. In her free time, you can find her in her sewing room. She loves creating with fabrics and threads and designing projects of her own. If you want to learn more about her projects, visit her at thecharmingneedle.com.

Candy Table Runner

BY CAROL ZENTGRAF

Everyone loves candy at the holidays, and this trio of appliquéd peppermints won't add any calories to the festivities. You can adapt the pattern to make any size, from a single candy for a placemat to a long runner with multiple candies on each side.

Materials

Use colors listed to create the classic "candy" look or use desired colors for a different effect.

- ☐ ½ yd (46 cm) of 45" (114.5 cm) wide cotton for runner top (A; shown: white tone-on-tone)

- ☐ ½ yd (68.5 cm) of 45" (114.5 cm) wide cotton print for runner bottom and appliqués (B; shown: red)

- ☐ ¼ yd (23 cm) each of two 45" (114.5 cm) wide cotton prints for appliqués (C and D; shown: green and bright green)

- ☐ 13½" × 35½" (34.5 × 90 cm) rectangle of low-loft batting

- ☐ ½ yd (46 cm) of ¼" (6 mm) wide satin ribbon (shown: red)

- ☐ ¾ yd (68.5 cm) of 18" (45.5 cm) wide double-stick fusible web

- ☐ ½ yd (46 cm) of ¼" (6 mm) wide double-stick fusible web tape

- ☐ Matching all-purpose and rayon threads

- ☐ Handsewing needle

- ☐ Candy Table Runner templates on page 35

Finished Size

12½" × 34½" (31.5 × 87.5 cm)

Notes

* All seam allowances are ½" (1.3 cm) unless otherwise noted; sew seams with right sides together.

* For explanations of terms and techniques, see Sewing Basics.

* The appliqué patterns have been reversed for tracing, and the appliqués will swirl in the opposite direction from the pattern when applied.

Cut and Prepare the Fabric

1 Photocopy the templates provided on page 35, following enlargement instructions. Cut 1 Runner Front each from fabric A and the batting.

2 Trace the swirling appliqué pieces from the Runner Front pattern onto the paper backing of the fusible web, grouping them by fabric color. The pieces are labeled with a letter corresponding to the fabric (B, C, or D) and a number; label each shape while tracing to avoid confusion when assembling the runner.

3 Cut 2 Runner Backs (cut 1, cut 1 reverse) from fabric B.

4 Following the manufacturer's instructions, adhere the fusible web to the wrong side of fabrics C and D and the remaining fabric B. Cut out the appliqués along the traced outlines.

Assemble the Runner

5 Remove the paper backing from one appliqué at a time and position it on the Runner Front, using the placement diagram on page 34 as a guide. When all the appliqués for one circle are in place, with their points meeting at the center, fuse the appliqués to the Runner Front. Continue until all the appliqués are fused in place.

6 Set the sewing machine for a zigzag stitch 2.5 mm wide and 1.0 mm long. With matching or coordinating thread, zigzag the edges of each appliqué piece, positioning the stitch so the right swing of the needle falls in the background fabric just beyond the appliqué edge.

7 Sew the straight edges of the Runner Backs together, leaving a 5" (12.5 cm) opening in the center of the seam. Press the seam allowances open.

8 Layer the pieces in the following order: assembled runner back (right-side up), the prepared runner front (right-side down), and the batting. Pin, then stitch the layers together. Stitch to the dot at each inside corner, pivot with the needle down, and take two stitches across the dot. Pivot again and continue sewing along the next segment of the curve. Trim the seam allowances to

¼" (6 mm) and clip the inside curves to the dots, taking care not to clip the stitches. Turn the runner right-side out through the opening in the runner back and press. Slip-stitch the opening closed.

9 Cut the ribbon in half and apply fusible web tape to the wrong side of each ribbon length. Center the ribbons along the side curves of the center candy on the runner front (indicated by dashed lines on the pattern; refer to the photo above for assistance). Wrap the ribbon ends to the runner back and fuse in place. Thread the machine with red rayon thread and set it for a zigzag stitch 2 mm long and 5 mm wide, slightly narrower than the ribbon width. Stitch along the center of each ribbon, couching it in place. The ribbon ends on the runner back should be caught by the stitches.

Credits

Fairfield Processing Corp., poly-fil.com, provided the Poly-fil low-loft batting.

Michael Miller Fabrics, michaelmiller fabrics.com, provided the cotton print fabrics.

Sulky of America, sulky.com, provided the 40 wt rayon thread.

The Warm Company, warmcompany.com, provided the Steam-A-Seam 2 fusible web sheets and tape. 🖋

- -

CAROL ZENTGRAF is a writer, designer, and editor specializing in sewing, embroidery, textiles, painting, and decorating. She designs for several magazines and fabric company websites. Carol is also the author of seven home décor sewing books.

placement diagram

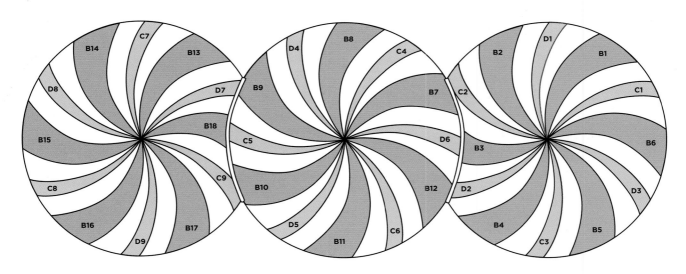

Enlarge both templates 400%

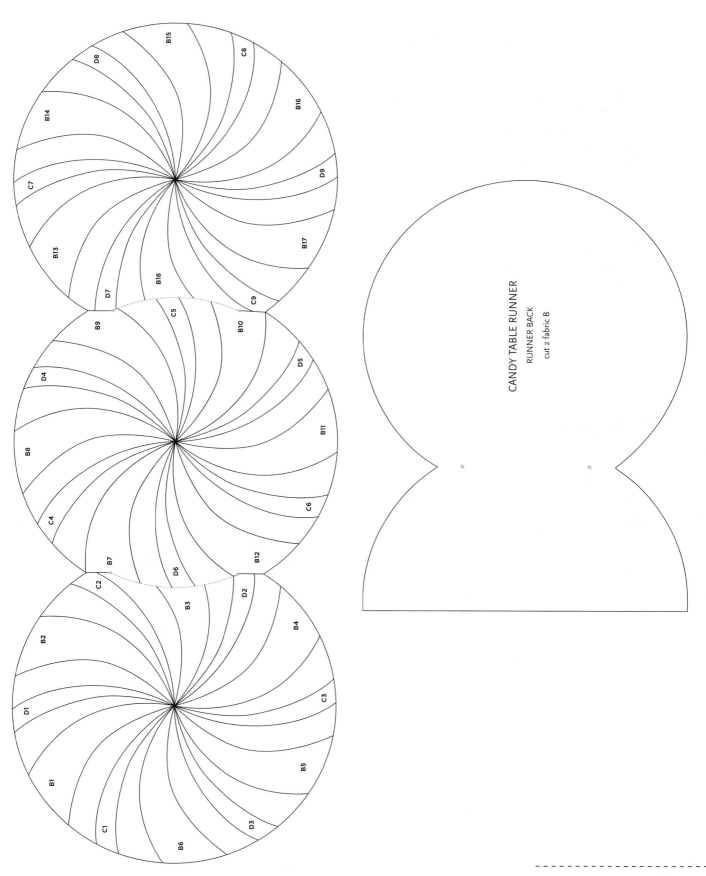

CANDY TABLE RUNNER
RUNNER BACK
cut 2 fabric B

Contemporary Table Runner

BY VIVIKA HANSEN DENEGRE

This trendy table runner showcases beautiful fabrics and easy techniques. It can be made in just a few hours with a small stash of fresh, contemporary fabrics. I used fabrics from Moda's "Modern Workshop" collection. This project is "fat quarter friendly" and appropriate for quilters of all levels of expertise. (A fat quarter is an 18" × 20"–22" cut of fabric.)

Materials

☐ 1 fat quarter to be used as the border for the 3 center blocks

☐ 6 assorted fabrics at least 10" × 10" (25.5 × 25.5 cm) (or fat quarters) for the 5" (12.5 cm) squares

☐ Backing fabric, 16" × 48" (40.5 × 122 cm) (pieced)

☐ Batting, 16" × 48" (40.5 × 122 cm)

☐ Spray starch

Finished Size

11½" × 41½" (29 × 105.5 cm)

Cut the Fabric

1 Cut the following from the block border fabric:

—5 strips 2½" × 20" (6.5 × 51 cm)

and subcut them into:

—6 rectangles 2½" × 5" (6.5 × 12.5 cm)

—6 rectangles 2½" × 9" (6.5 × 23 cm)

From the assorted fabrics, cut:

—11 squares 5" × 5" (12.5 × 12.5 cm)

—2 squares 3" × 3" (7.5 × 7.5 cm)

—22 strips 1" × 7" (2.5 × 18 cm) (cut matching pairs)

Make the Topstitched X's

2 Fold a 1" (2.5 cm) wide strip lengthwise to just beyond the center of the strip. Press with starch to create a crisp crease. Fold the other side of the strip (being careful not to bring the raw edge beyond the previously ironed crease) and press again. Repeat for all of the 1" (2.5 cm) strips.

3 Cut the starched strips into 6" (15 cm) lengths. Arrange 2 matching strips into an "X" shape on each 5" (12.5 cm) square. Pinning is not necessary.

4 Making sure the strips are raw-edge down, topstitch them in place on both sides using a topstitch foot (Bernina #5 or #10) and a slightly elongated straight stitch. This is a good place to showcase a shiny rayon or polyester thread.

Piece the Blocks

5 Choose three 5" (12.5 cm) squares to be the center blocks of the runner.

6 Sew one 5" × 2½" (12.5 × 6.5 cm) strip of main fabric to opposite sides of each square. Press the seam allowance away from the center.

7 Sew one 9" × 2½" (23 × 6.5 cm) strip of main fabric to the 2 remaining sides of each block. Press the seam allowance away from the center.

Assemble the Runner

Note: There are two different units in this runner and five diagonal rows.

8 Using the photograph as a guide, arrange the fabrics for the runner.

9 Unit 1 (diagonal rows 1 and 5): Starting at the top, sew a 3" (7.5 cm) square to the lower right corner of the top 5" (12.5 cm) square. Press the seam allowance toward the larger square. Repeat with the bottom squares.

10 Unit 2 (diagonal rows 2–4): Sew one 5" (12.5 cm) square to the upper right edge of the 9" (23 cm) block, and one 5" (12.5 cm) square to the lower left edge of the block. Press the seams toward the smaller squares. Repeat for the remaining blocks.

11 Sew all of the units together in order from top to bottom, staggering them as shown and nesting the seams. Press all of the seams toward the top of the runner.

Finish the Runner

12 Place the backing fabric right-side up on the batting. Center the runner on top of the backing fabric, right sides together, and pin all points.

13 Using matching thread and starting in the middle of a long side, sew with ¼" (6 mm) seams around the entire piece, leaving a 6"–8" (15–20.5 cm) opening for turning. Make a 90-degree turn at every inside and outside corner to ensure a sharp edge on the runner.

14 Trim away the excess backing and batting to match the top of the runner.

15 Trim the tip of every outside corner straight across the top to ensure a sharp corner and to ease the bulk. Be sure not to cut the stitching thread. Cut a ¼" (6 mm) slit in the inside corners down to the stitching line to ease turning. Again, be sure not to cut the stitching thread.

16 Turn the piece right-side out. Using a knitting needle, gently push the edge of every corner until it is sharp. Press the edges, and handstitch the opening closed.

17 Stitch in the ditch of all seams and around the topstitched elements. ✍

- -

VIVIKA HANSEN DENEGRE is the editor of *Quilting Arts Magazine*.

Windows Improv
Table Runner and Placemat

BY MALKA DUBRAWSKY

Improvisational cutting and piecing give this patchwork table runner and placemat fresh design. With key elements of the blocks aligned, the pattern still comes through so you can enjoy quilting your own inspired mix of colorful fabrics.

Materials

□ ½ yd (46 cm) of 45" (115 cm) wide cotton in cream or white for binding and piecing

□ 1⅛ yd (1 m) of 45" (115 cm) wide coordinating fabric for backing

□ 25–30 assorted, primarily solid color, cotton and linen scraps, each large enough for cutting 1 or 2 squares 3" (7.5 cm) or larger

□ 25–30 assorted, primarily solid color, cotton or linen strips, each measuring at least 1½" (3.8 cm) wide and long enough to cut 2 or 4 strips up to 4½" (11.4 cm) long

□ Coordinating sewing and quilting thread(s)

□ Crib-size (45" × 60" [115 × 153 cm]) cotton batting

□ Quilter's clear acrylic ruler

□ Rotary cutter, self-healing mat, and rigid gridded acrylic ruler (optional but recommended)

□ Safety pins or quilt basting spray

□ Handsewing needle

Finished Size

16" × 50" (40.5 × 127 cm)

Notes

∗ All seam allowances are ¼" (6 mm) unless otherwise indicated.

∗ For explanations of terms and techniques, see Sewing Basics.

∗ Each patchwork block is composed of a freehand-cut square and 2 or more freehand-cut strips.

∗ Press all patchwork seams to one side, alternating sides where seams intersect.

Cut Fabric

1 Cut 4 strips 1½" (3.8 cm) wide, across the width of the binding fabric. Refer to Create Binding in Sewing Basics to join the strips and prepare the binding (refer to option A for folding). Set it aside for Step 25.

2 From the remaining binding fabric, free-hand cut strips at least 1½" (3.8 cm) wide; use all the remaining fabric and cut as many strips as possible.

3 From the backing fabric, cut two 18" × 44" (45.5 × 112 cm) pieces. Set aside.

4 From the assorted cotton and linen fabrics, cut a variety of strips and squares. Either cut the shapes freehand, with scissors, or use a rotary cutter and mat, but strive to keep variations in width a part of the cutting process. For each of the 48 blocks, you'll need to cut a square roughly 3" (7.5 cm) on a side and a strip roughly 1½" wide × 8" long (3.8 × 20.3 cm). Keep the strips of binding fabric separate to use in evening up the blocks before assembling them.

Create First Patchwork Block

Use the various freehand-cut squares and strips for the following instructions.

5 Pin a strip to one edge of a square right sides together, matching the raw edges at one end of the strip. Sew, then press the seam to one side. Trim the strip so it is even with the square.

6 Pin the remaining length of the strip, or a second strip, to an adjacent side of the same square right sides together, so that the second strip is perpendicular to the first strip. Sew, press,

and trim as before. You now have 1 completed block (FIGURE 1).

7 Repeat Steps 5 and 6 to make 47 more blocks.

8 As you join the blocks, the inner seam lines (between the square and the strip) should align in adjacent blocks. If necessary, add binding fabric strips (cut in Step 2) to alter the width of a block so both the raw edges and the inner seams of the blocks align. See FIGURE 2 for an example of the relationship between adjacent blocks. Notice that the interior seams match and that the lower block has been widened with a binding fabric strip to match the upper block's width. Sew the 2 blocks together, press seam allowances to one side, and trim any excess length or width from the binding fabric strip.

9 Find 2 more blocks with squares the same height as the first 2. Repeat Step 8 to join them, making a second pair of blocks. If necessary, extend both the length and the width of a block so it fits into the group.

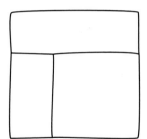

figure 1

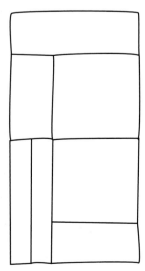

figure 2

10 Pin the pairs of blocks right sides together along one long edge, matching the internal seams and the seams between blocks, and sew together (see **FIGURE 3**). Trim any overhanging edges and press the seam allowances to one side. You have now created the center 4-patch unit.

For the next steps, place the patches as directed but do not sew yet. Remember to add the binding fabric strips as necessary to ensure that the blocks' widths match as you add each new block.

11 Working on a design wall or tabletop and referring to **FIGURE 4**, place 2 more patches so they abut the central 4-block unit along one corner, making sure the new blocks' squares and strips are positioned as shown.

12 Referring to **FIGURE 5,** place a block into the corner of the unit, orienting the new block's square and strips as shown.

13 Referring to **FIGURES 6, 7,** and **8,** add blocks as shown. Three new blocks are added in each figure, completing a border around the original 4-block unit.

14 Visualize the arrangement as a row of blocks along each side of the center 4-block unit. Beginning with one of the rows to the left or right of the center unit, place 2 patches right sides together, aligning the raw edges that were adjacent in the arrangement. Sew those edges together, press the seam allowances to one side, and trim (if necessary) as before. Continue to attach the patches in this manner until you have created a 4-block row.

15 Repeat Step 14 with the 4-block row on the opposite side. Then, repeat with each of the 2-block rows (at the top and bottom of the center 4-block unit).

16 Sew one of the 2-block rows to the center unit, press, and trim (if necessary) as before. Repeat to attach the second 2-block row, then add a 4-block row to each side of the unit.

Sew Remaining Patchwork Blocks

17 Repeat Steps 5–16 twice to assemble a total of 3 units, each containing 16 blocks and as many additional binding fabric strips as necessary.

18 Pin 2 units right sides together along one edge. Sew together and press the seam allowances to one side. Repeat to attach the remaining unit, making a 3-unit runner.

Finish Table Runner

19 From the cotton batting, cut a rectangle measuring 20" × 60" (51 × 152.5 cm); set aside.

20 Pin the 18" × 44" (45.5 × 112 cm) backing pieces, right sides together, along one short edge. Sew together and then press the seam open.

21 Lay the assembled backing, wrong-side up, on a flat surface. Smooth the batting in place on top at one end of the backing fabric. Trim away the excess backing so it matches the batting length. Lay the pieced top right-side up on the batting, centering it.

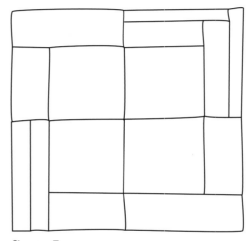

figure 3

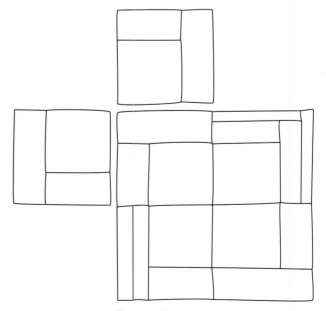

figure 4

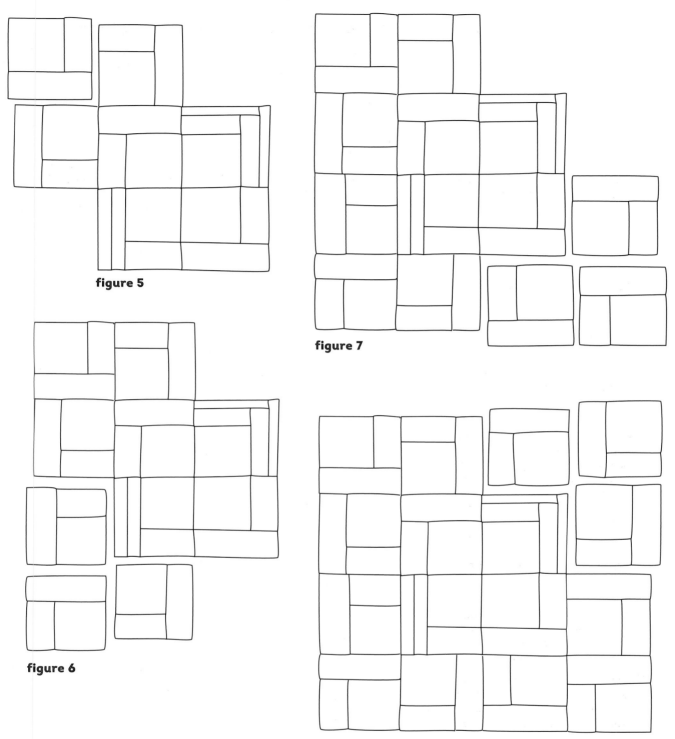

figure 5

figure 6

figure 7

figure 8

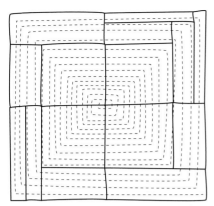

figure 9

22 Use safety pins spaced 4"–6" (10–15 cm) apart to baste the 3 layers together, or apply quilt basting spray, following the manufacturer's instructions.

Machine or hand quilt the layers together as desired, removing the basting pins as you work. To create a similar look to the quilting shown here, stitch concentric squares on each of the 4-block center units and concentric 2-sided angles on the surrounding blocks (see **FIGURE 9**).

Square up the quilt (see Sewing Basics).

Using the binding created earlier, follow the instructions under Binding with Mitered Corners, see Sewing Basics to bind the quilt, being sure to miter the corners for a clean, neat finish. 🍃

MALKA DUBRAWSKY crafts and dyes fabric from her home in Austin, Texas. She is the author of *Fresh Quilting* and *Color Your Cloth: A Quilter's Guide to Dyeing and Patterning Fabric.* Read her musings at stitchindye.blogspot.com.

Variation: Placemat

Why not create fabulous patchwork placemats to go with your beautiful new table runner? To make a placemat, cut 2 strips for binding and set them aside, then simply repeat Steps 5–16 to create one patchwork unit. Follow Steps 21–25 to assemble, quilt, and bind the placemat. Easy!

Finished Size

About 18" (46 cm) square. (The size will vary, depending on the squares and strips used in assembly.)

Fabric

(for 1 placemat)

- ☐ 8–10 assorted, primarily solid color, cotton and linen scraps, each large enough for cutting 1 or 2 squares 3" (7.5 cm) or larger

- ☐ 8–10 assorted, primarily solid color, cotton or linen strips, each measuring at least 1½" (3.8 cm) wide and long enough to cut 2 or 4 strips up to 4½" (11.5 cm) long

- ☐ ¼ yd (23 cm) of 45" (115 cm) wide cotton in cream or white for binding and piecing

- ☐ 20" (51 cm) square of cotton batting. (You'll have enough left over from the table runner.)

- ☐ 20" (51 cm) square of coordinating fabric for backing

Sewing Basics

A quick reference guide to basic tools, techniques, and terms

For all projects (unless otherwise indicated):

* When piecing: Use ¼" (6 mm) seam allowances. Stitch with the right sides together. After stitching a seam, press it to set the seam; then open the fabrics and press the seam allowance toward the darker fabric.

* Yardages are based upon 44" (112 cm) wide fabric.

Sewing Kit

The following items are essential for your sewing kit. Make sure you have these tools on hand before starting any of the projects:

* **ACRYLIC RULER** This is a clear flat ruler, with a measuring grid at least 2" × 18" (5 × 45.5 cm). A rigid acrylic (quilter's) ruler should be used when working with a rotary cutter. You should have a variety of rulers in different shapes and sizes.

* **BATTING** 100% cotton, 100% wool, plus bamboo, silk, and blends.

* **BONE FOLDER** Allows you to make non-permanent creases in fabric, paper, and other materials.

* **CRAFT SCISSORS** To use when cutting out paper patterns.

* **EMBROIDERY SCISSORS** These small scissors are used to trim off threads, clip corners, and do other intricate cutting work.

* **FABRIC** Commercial prints, hand-dyes, cottons, upholstery, silks, wools; the greater the variety of types, colors, designs, and textures, the better.

* **FABRIC MARKING PENS/PENCILS + TAILOR'S CHALK** Available in several colors for use on light and dark fabrics; use to trace patterns and pattern markings onto your fabric. Tailor's chalk is available in triangular pieces, rollers, and pencils. Some forms (such as powdered) can simply be brushed away; refer to the manufacturer's instructions for the recommended removal method for your chosen marking tool.

* **FREE-MOTION OR DARNING FOOT** Used to free-motion quilt.

* **FUSIBLE WEB** Used to fuse fabrics together. There are a variety of products on the market.

* **GLUE** Glue stick, fabric glue, and all-purpose glue.

* **HANDSEWING + EMBROIDERY NEEDLES** Keep an assortment of sewing and embroidery needles in different sizes, from fine to sturdy.

* **IRON, IRONING BOARD + PRESS CLOTHS** An iron is an essential tool when sewing. Use cotton muslin or silk organza as a press cloth to protect delicate fabric surfaces from direct heat. Use a Teflon sheet or parchment paper to protect your iron and ironing board when working with fusible web.

* **MEASURING TAPE** Make sure it's at least 60" (152.5 cm) long and retractable.

* **NEEDLE THREADER** An inexpensive aid to make threading the eye of the needle superfast.

* **PINKING SHEARS** These shears have notched teeth that leave a zigzag edge on the cut cloth to prevent fraying.

* **POINT TURNER** A blunt, pointed tool that helps push out the corners of a project and/or smooth seams. A knitting needle or chopstick may also be used.

* **ROTARY CUTTER + SELF-HEALING MAT** Useful for cutting out fabric quickly. Always use a mat to protect the blade and your work surface (a rigid acrylic ruler should be used with a rotary cutter to make straight cuts).

* **SAFETY PINS** Always have a bunch on hand.

* **SCISSORS + SHEARS** Heavy-duty shears reserved for fabric only; a pair of small, sharp embroidery scissors; thread snips; a pair of all-purpose scissors; pinking shears.

* **SEAM RIPPER** Handy for quickly ripping out stitches.

* **SEWING MACHINE** With free-motion capabilities.

* **STRAIGHT PINS + PINCUSHION** Always keep lots of pins nearby.

* **TEMPLATE SUPPLIES** Keep freezer paper or other large paper (such as parchment paper) on hand for tracing the templates you intend to use. Regular office paper may be used for templates that will fit. You should also have card stock or plastic if you wish to make permanent templates that can be reused.

* **THIMBLE** Your fingers and thumbs will thank you.

* **THREAD** All types, including hand and machine thread for stitching and quilting; variegated; metallic; 100% cotton; monofilament.

* **ZIPPER FOOT** An accessory foot for your machine with a narrow profile that can be positioned to sew close to the zipper teeth. A zipper foot is adjustable so the foot can be moved to either side of the needle.

Glossary of Sewing Terms and Techniques

BACKSTITCH Stitching in reverse for a short distance at the beginning and end of a seam line to secure the stitches. Most machines have a button or knob for this function (also called backtack).

BASTING Using long, loose stitches to hold something in place temporarily. To baste by machine, use the longest straight stitch length available on your machine. To baste by hand, use stitches at least 1/4" (6 mm) long. Use a contrasting thread to make the stitches easier to spot for removal.

BIAS The direction across a fabric that is located at a 45-degree angle from the lengthwise or crosswise grain. The bias has high stretch and a very fluid drape.

BIAS TAPE Made from fabric strips cut on a 45-degree angle to the grainline, the bias cut creates an edging fabric that will stretch to enclose smooth or curved edges. You can buy bias tape ready-made or make your own.

CLIPPING CURVES Involves cutting tiny slits or triangles into the seam allowance of curved edges so the seam will lie flat when turned right-side out. Cut slits along concave curves and triangles (with points toward the seam line) along a convex curve. Be careful not to clip into the stitches.

CLIP THE CORNERS Clipping the corners of a project reduces bulk and allows for crisper corners in the finished project. To clip a corner, cut off a triangle-shaped piece of fabric across the seam allowances at the corner. Cut close to the seam line but be careful not to cut through the stitches.

DART This stitched triangular fold is used to give shape and form to the fabric to fit body curves.

EDGESTITCH A row of topstitching placed very close (1/16"–1/8" [2–3 mm]) to an edge or an existing seam line.

FABRIC GRAIN The grain is created in a woven fabric by the threads that travel lengthwise and crosswise. The lengthwise grain runs parallel to the selvedges; the crosswise grain should always be perpendicular to the lengthwise threads. If the grains aren't completely straight and perpendicular, grasp the fabric at

diagonally opposite corners and pull gently to restore the grain. In knit fabrics, the lengthwise grain runs along the wales (ribs), parallel to the selvedges, with the crosswise grain running along the courses (perpendicular to the wales).

FINGER-PRESS Pressing a fold or crease with your fingers as opposed to using an iron.

FUSSY-CUT Cutting a specific motif from a commercial or hand-printed fabric. Generally used to center a motif in a patchwork pattern or to feature a specific motif in an appliqué design. Use a clear acrylic ruler or template plastic to isolate the selected motif and ensure that it will fit within the desired size, including seam allowances.

GRAINLINE A pattern marking showing the direction of the grain. Make sure the grainline marked on the pattern runs parallel to the lengthwise grain of your fabric, unless the grainline is specifically marked as crosswise or bias.

INTERFACING Material used to stabilize or reinforce fabrics. Fusible interfacing has an adhesive coating on one side that adheres to fabric when ironed.

LINING The inner fabric of a garment or bag, used to create a finished interior that covers the raw edges of the seams.

MITER Joining a seam or fold at an angle that bisects the project corner. Most common is a 45-degree angle, like a picture frame, but shapes other than squares or rectangles will have miters with different angles.

OVERCAST STITCH A machine stitch that wraps around the fabric raw edge to finish edges and prevent unraveling. Some sewing machines have several overcast stitch options; consult your sewing machine manual for information on stitch settings and the appropriate presser foot for the chosen stitch (often the standard presser foot can be used). A zigzag stitch can be used as an alternative to finish raw edges if your machine doesn't have an overcast stitch function.

PRESHRINK Many fabrics shrink when washed; you need to wash, dry, and press all your fabric before you start to sew, following the suggested cleaning method marked on the fabric bolt (keep in mind that the appropriate cleaning method

may not be machine washing). Don't skip this step!

RIGHT SIDE The front side, or the side that should be on the outside of a finished garment. On a print fabric, the print will be stronger on the right side of the fabric.

RIGHT SIDES TOGETHER The right sides of two fabric layers should be facing each other.

SATIN STITCH (MACHINE) This is a smooth, completely filled column of zigzag stitches achieved by setting the stitch length short enough for complete coverage but long enough to prevent bunching and thread buildup.

SEAM ALLOWANCE The amount of fabric between the raw edge and the seam.

SELVEDGE This is the tightly woven border on the lengthwise edges of woven fabric and the finished lengthwise edges of knit fabric.

SQUARING UP After you have pieced together a fabric block or section, check to make sure the edges are straight and the measurements are correct. Use a rotary cutter and an acrylic ruler to trim the block if necessary.

STITCH IN THE DITCH Lay the quilt sandwich right-side up under the presser foot and sew along the seam line "ditch." The stitches will fall between the two fabric pieces and disappear into the seam.

TOPSTITCH Used to hold pieces firmly in place and/or to add a decorative effect, a topstitch is simply a stitch that can be seen on the outside of the garment or piece. To topstitch, make a line of stitching on the outside (right side) of the piece, usually a set distance from an existing seam.

UNDERSTITCHING A line of stitches placed on a facing (or lining), very near the facing/garment seam. Understitching is used to hold the seam allowances and facing together and to prevent the facing from rolling toward the outside of the garment.

WRONG SIDE The wrong side of the fabric is the underside, or the side that should be on the inside of a finished garment. On a print fabric, the print will be lighter or less obvious on the wrong side of the fabric.

Stitch Glossary

BACKSTITCH

Working from right to left, bring the needle up at **1** and insert behind the starting point at **2**. Bring the needle up at **3**; repeat by inserting at **1** and bringing the needle up at a point that is a stitch length beyond **3**.

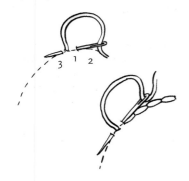

BASTING STITCH

Using the longest straight stitch length on your machine, baste to temporarily hold fabric layers and seams in position for final stitching. It can also be done by hand. When basting, use a contrasting thread to make it easier to spot when you're taking it out.

BLANKET STITCH

Working from left to right, bring the needle up at **1** and insert at **2**. Bring the needle back up at **3** and over the working thread. Repeat by making the next stitch in the same manner, keeping the spacing even.

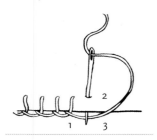

BLINDSTITCH/BLIND-HEM STITCH

Used mainly for hemming fabrics where an inconspicuous hem is difficult to achieve (this stitch is also useful for securing binding on the wrong side). Fold the hem edge back about ¼" (6 mm). Take a small stitch in the garment, picking up only a few threads of the fabric, then take the next stitch ¼" (6 mm) ahead in the hem. Continue, alternating stitches between the hem and the garment (if using for a non-hemming application, simply alternate stitches between the two fabric edges being joined).

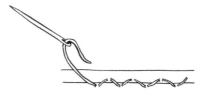

CHAIN STITCH

Working from top to bottom, bring the needle up at and reinsert at **1** to create a loop; do not pull the thread taut. Bring the needle back up at **2**, keeping the needle above the loop and gently pulling the needle toward you to tighten the loop flush to the fabric. Repeat by inserting the needle at **2** to form a loop and bring the needle up at **3**. Tack the last loop down with a straight stitch.

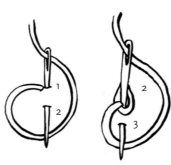

STRAIGHT STITCH + RUNNING STITCH

Working from right to left, make a straight stitch by bringing the needle up and insert at **1**, ⅛"–¼" (3–6 mm) from the starting point. To make a line of running stitches (a row of straight stitches worked one after the other), bring the needle up at **2** and repeat.

FRENCH KNOT

Bring the needle up at **1** and hold the thread taut above the fabric. Point the needle toward your fingers and move the needle in a circular motion to wrap the thread around the needle once or twice. Insert the needle near **1** and hold the thread taut near the knot as you pull the needle and thread through the knot and the fabric to complete.

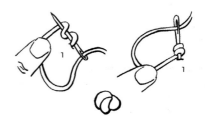

COUCHING

Working from right to left, use one thread, known as the couching or working thread, to tack down one or more strands of fiber, known as the couched fibers. Bring the working thread up at **1** and insert at **2**, over the fibers to tack them down, bringing the needle back up at **3**. The fibers are now encircled by the couching thread. Repeat to couch the desired length of fiber(s). This stitch may also be worked from left to right, and the spacing between the couching threads may vary for different design effects.

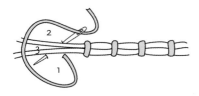

CROSS-STITCH

Working from right to left, bring the needle up at **1**, insert at **2**, then bring the needle back up at **3**. Finish by inserting the needle at **4**. Repeat for the desired number of stitches.

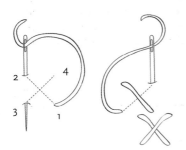

WHIPSTITCH

Bring the needle up at **1**, insert at **2**, and bring up at **3**. These quick stitches do not have to be very tight or close together.

STANDARD HAND-APPLIQUÉ STITCH

Cut a length of thread 12"–18" (30.5–45.5 cm). Thread the newly cut end through the eye of the needle, pull this end through, and knot it. Use this technique to thread the needle and knot the thread to help keep the thread's "twist" intact and to reduce knotting. Beginning at the straightest edge of the appliqué and working from right to left, bring the needle up from the underside, through the background fabric and the very edge of the appliqué at **1**, catching only a few threads of the appliqué fabric. Pull the thread taut, then insert the needle into the background fabric at **2**, as close as possible to **1**. Bring the needle up through the background fabric at **3**, 1/8" (3 mm) beyond **2**. Continue in this manner, keeping the thread taut (do not pull it so tight that the fabric puckers) to keep the stitching as invisible as possible.

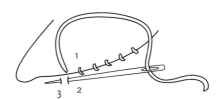

SLIP STITCH

Working from right to left, join two pieces of fabric by taking a 1/16"–1/4" (2–6 mm) long stitch into the folded edge of one piece of fabric and bringing the needle out. Insert the needle into the folded edge of the other piece of fabric, directly across from the point where the thread emerged from the previous stitch. Repeat by inserting the needle into the first piece of fabric. The thread will be almost entirely hidden inside the folds of the fabrics.

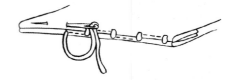

Create Binding

CUTTING STRAIGHT STRIPS

Cut strips on the crosswise grain, from selvedge to selvedge. Use a rotary cutter and straightedge to obtain a straight cut. Remove the selvedges and join the strips with diagonal seams (see instructions at right).

CUTTING BIAS STRIPS

Fold one cut end of the fabric to meet one selvedge, forming a fold at a 45-degree angle to the selvedge (1). With the fabric placed on a self-healing mat, cut off the fold with a rotary cutter, using a straightedge as a guide to make a straight cut. With the straightedge and rotary cutter, cut strips to the appropriate width (2). Join the strips with diagonal seams.

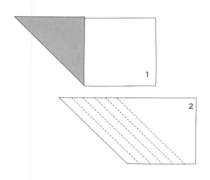

BINDING WITH MITERED CORNERS

Decide whether you will use a Double-fold Binding (option A at right) or a Double-layer Binding (option B at right). *If using double-layer binding follow the alternate italicized instructions in parenthesis.*

Open the binding and press ½" (1.3 cm) to the wrong side at one short end *(refold the binding at the center crease and proceed)*. Starting with the folded-under end of the binding, place it near the center of the first edge of the project to be bound, matching the raw edges, and pin in place. Begin sewing near the center of one edge of the project, along the first crease *(at the appropriate distance from the raw edge)*, leaving several inches of the binding fabric free at the beginning. Stop sewing ¼" (6 mm) before reaching the corner, backstitch, and cut the threads. Rotate the project 90 degrees to position it for sewing the next side. Fold the binding fabric up, away from the project, at a 45-degree angle (1), then fold it back

down along the project raw edge (2). This forms a miter at the corner. Stitch the second side, beginning at the project raw edge (2) and ending ¼" (6 mm) from the next corner, as before.

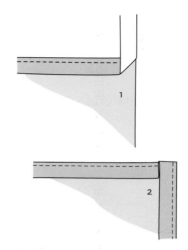

Continue as established until you have completed the last corner. Continue stitching until you are a few inches from the beginning edge of the binding fabric. Overlap the pressed beginning edge of the binding by ½" (1.3 cm) (or overlap more as necessary for security) and trim the working edge to fit. Finish sewing the binding *(opening the center fold and tucking the raw edge inside the pressed end of the binding strip)*. Refold the binding along all the creases and then fold it over the project raw edges to the back, enclosing the raw edges *(there are no creases to worry about with option B)*. The folded edge of the binding strip should just cover the stitches visible on the project back. Slip-stitch or blindstitch the binding in place, tucking in the corners to complete the miters as you go (3).

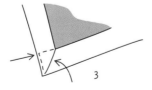

DIAGONAL SEAMS FOR JOINING STRIPS

Lay two strips right sides together, at right angles. The area where the strips overlap forms a square. Sew diagonally across the square as shown above. Trim the excess fabric ¼" (6 mm) away from the seam line and press the seam allowances open. Repeat to join all the strips, forming one long fabric band.

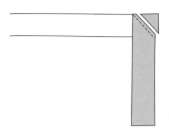

FOLD BINDING

A. Double-fold Binding

This option will create binding that is similar to packaged double-fold bias tape/binding. Fold the strip in half lengthwise, with wrong sides together; press. Open up the fold and then fold each long edge toward the wrong side, so that the raw edges meet in the middle (1). Refold the binding along the existing center crease, enclosing the raw edges (2), and press again.

B. Double-layer Binding

This option creates a double-thick binding with only one fold. This binding is often favored by quilters. Fold the strip in half lengthwise with wrong sides together; press.

Find popular patterns for quick and easy projects with these *Craft Tree* publications, brought to you by Interweave.

Colorful Projects for Outdoor Fun
ISBN 978-1-62033-561-1

Easy Quilting Projects
ISBN 978-1-62033-556-7

Easy Sewing Projects
ISBN 978-1-62033-558-1

Great Projects for Guys
ISBN 978-1-62033-559-8

More Teacher Gifts
ISBN 978-1-62033-560-4

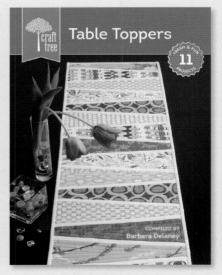

Table Toppers
ISBN 978-1-62033-557-4

Visit your favorite retailer or order online at
interweavestore.com

INTERWEAVE.
interweavestore.com